THE COLOR OF CREATION

St. John Paul II — an artist himself — kicked off his 1999 Letter to Artists with this familiar line from Genesis 1:31: “God saw all that he had made, and it was very good.”

He did this, pointing to the very beginning of salvation history’s tale, to draw the parallel that in our human desire for creativity, we inherently sense “some echo of the mystery of creation with which God, the sole creator of all things, has wished in some way to associate you.”

Whether through growing families, daily labor, strengthening the Church, or simply through the use of colored pencils on paper, we as children of God have an innate desire to partake in God’s creative nature.

It is our hope that this series of Adult Coloring Journals helps you tap into that desire to experience creativity with God. It is for this reason that we designed these not just as part of a recent fad but also as tools to draw you deeper into prayer and Scripture along with the very mystery of creation that God desires to share with you.

Now go create with God!

28 27 26 25 24 3 4 5 6 7 8 9

Our Sunday Visitor Publishing Division
Our Sunday Visitor, Inc.
200 Noll Plaza
Huntington, IN 46750
1-800-348-2440

ISBN: 978-1-68192-084-9 (Inventory No. T1826)

Cover design: Tyler Ottinger
Cover art: Shutterstock.com
Interior design: Tyler Ottinger

Interior art Shutterstock.com: OlichO, DT10, Anna_Zubkova, Marina Demidova, Franzi, totallypic, Ivala, Julia Snegireva, Julia Snegireva, Catherine Glazkova, IrinaKrivoruchko, Lexver, Franzi, Helen Lane, Franzi, Lexver, Anna_Zubkova, Marina Demidova, OlichO, Marina Demidova, OlichO, OlichO, OlichO, OlichO, OlichO, Helen Lane, Helen Lane, Helen Lane, Helen Lane, Helen Lane, OlichO, OlichO, OlichO, OlichO, OlichO, OlichO, OlichO, Maroshka, Lexver, Toporovska Nataliia, Lexver, Helen Lane

PRINTED IN THE UNITED STATES OF AMERICA

Most high, all powerful, all good Lord!
All praise is Yours, all glory, all honor, and all blessing.

"In the beginning God created the heavens and the earth."

— Genesis 1:1

To You, alone, Most High, do they belong.
No mortal lips are worthy to pronounce Your name.

"Each little flower that opens, each little bird that sings, he made their glowing colors, he made their tiny wings." — Cecil Frances Alexander

Be praised, my Lord, through all Your creatures,
especially through my lord Brother Sun,
who brings the day; and You give light through him.
And he is beautiful and radiant in all his splendor!
Of You, Most High, he bears the likeness.

"All things bright and beautiful, all creatures great and small, all things wise and wonderful, the Lord God made them all." — *Cecil Frances Alexander*

Be praised, my Lord, through Sister Moon and the stars;
in the heavens You have made them bright, precious
and beautiful.

Let the whole creation cry, "Glory to the Lord on high!"
Heaven and earth, awake and sing, "Praise to our almighty King!"
Praise him, angel hosts above, ever bright and fair in love;
Sun and moon, lift up your voice; night and star in God rejoice.
Alleluia! — Stopford A. Brooke

Be praised, my Lord, through Brothers Wind and Air,
and clouds and storms, and all the weather,
through which You give Your creatures sustenance.

"The whole earth is a living icon of the face of God."

— St. John of Damascus

Be praised, my Lord, through Sister Water;
she is very useful, and humble, and precious, and pure.

"The aesthetic value of creation cannot be overlooked. Our very contact with nature has a deep restorative power; contemplation of its magnificence imparts peace and serenity. The Bible speaks again and again of the goodness and beauty of creation, which is called to glorify God." — St. John Paul II

Be praised, my Lord, through Brother Fire,
through whom You brighten the night.
He is beautiful and cheerful, and powerful and strong.

"Our insistence that each human being is an image of God should not make us overlook the fact that each creature has its own purpose. None is superfluous. The entire material universe speaks of God's love, his boundless affection for us. Soil, water, mountains: everything is, as it were, a caress of God."

— Pope Francis

Be praised, my Lord, through our sister Mother Earth,
who feeds us and rules us, and produces various fruits
with colored flowers and herbs.

"The universe unfolds in God, who fills it completely. Hence, there is a mystical meaning to be found in a leaf, in a mountain trail, in a dewdrop, in a poor person's face. The ideal is not only to pass from the exterior to the interior to discover the action of God in the soul, but also to discover God in all things."

— Pope Francis

Be praised, my Lord, through those who forgive for love of You; through those who endure sickness and trial.

"Contemplation deepens the more we feel the working of God's grace within our hearts, and the better we learn to encounter God in creatures outside ourselves."

— St. Bonaventure

Happy those who endure in peace,
for by You, Most High, they will be crowned.

"For not only, indeed, does the magnitude and beauty of the creation, but also the very manner of it, display a God who is the artificer of the universe.... He has made the mode of this creation to become our best teacher." — St. John Chrysostom

Be praised, my Lord, through our sister Bodily Death,
from whose embrace no living person can escape.
Woe to those who die in mortal sin!
Happy those she finds doing Your most holy will.
The second death can do no harm to them.

"Some people, to discover God, read books. But there is a great book: the very appearance of created things. Look above you! Look below you! Note it. Read it. God, whom you want to discover, never wrote that book with ink. Instead, he set before your eyes the things that he has made. Can you ask for a louder voice than that?

— attrib. St. Augustine

Praise and bless my Lord, and give thanks,
and serve Him with great humility.

"Ah Lord God! It is you who have made the heavens and the earth by your great power and by your outstretched arm! Nothing is too hard for you."

— Jeremiah 32:17

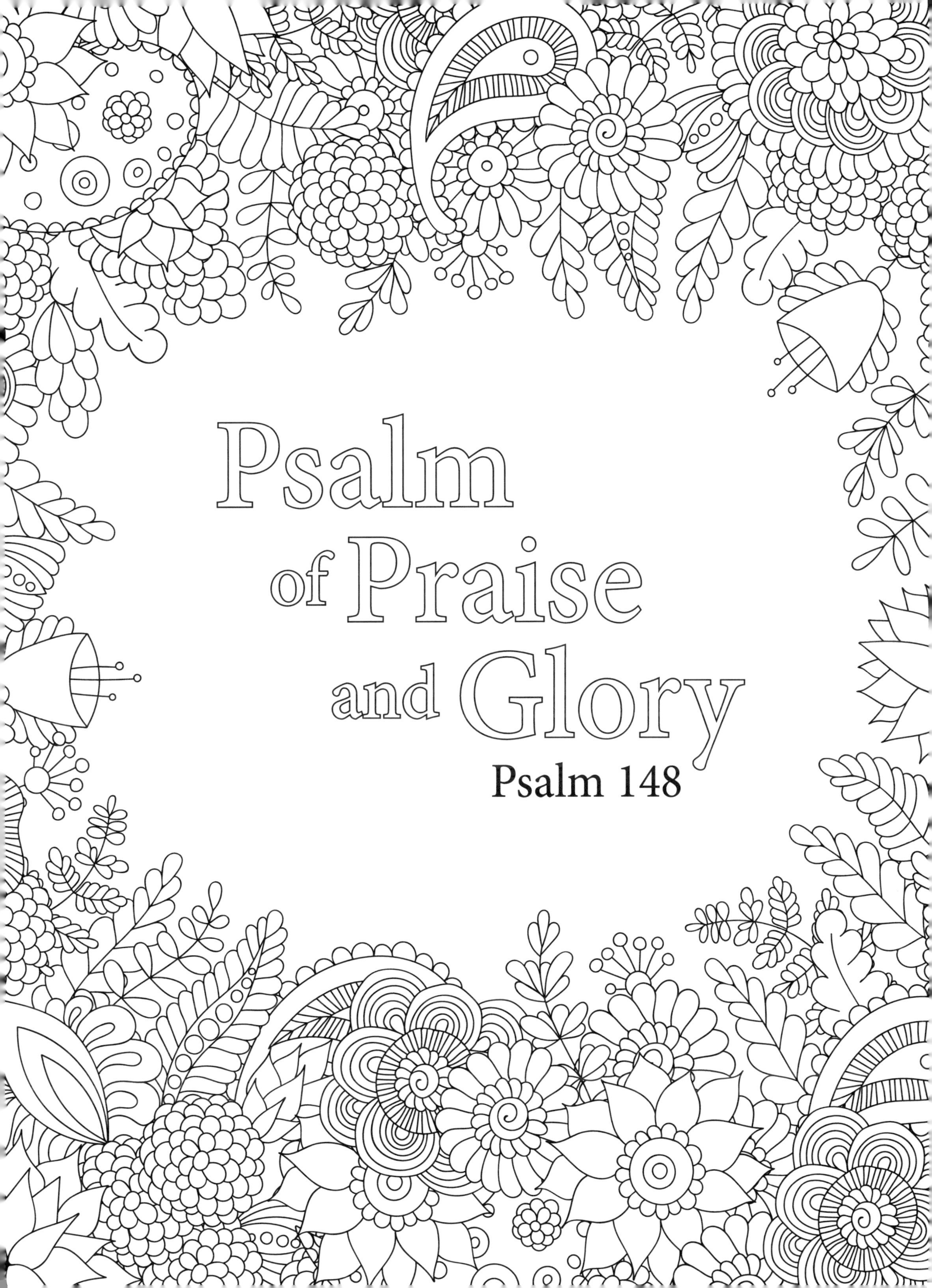
Psalm
of Praise
and Glory
Psalm 148

"Creation is a bible whose letters and syllables are the particular aspects of all creatures and whose words are the more universal aspects of creation."
— St. Maximus the Confessor

Praise the LORD!

Praise the LORD from the heavens,
praise him in the heights!

Praise him, all his angels,
praise him, all his host!

"God passes through the thicket of the world, and wherever his glance falls he turns all things to beauty." — St. John of the Cross

Praise him, sun and moon,
praise him, all you shining stars!

Praise him, you highest heavens,
and you waters above the heavens!

"Believe one who knows: You will find something greater in woods than in the books. Trees and stones will teach you that which you can never learn from masters."

— St. Bernard of Clairvaux

Let them praise the name of the LORD!
For he commanded and they were created.

And he established them for ever and ever;
he fixed their bounds which cannot be passed.

"To protect creation, to protect every man and every woman, to look upon them with tenderness and love, is to open up a horizon of hope; it is to let a shaft of light break through the heavy clouds; it is to bring the warmth of hope!" — Pope Francis

Praise the LORD from the earth,
 you sea monsters and all deeps,
fire and hail, snow and frost,
 stormy wind fulfilling his command!

"If there is anyone who is not enlightened by this sublime magnificence of created things, he is blind. If there is anyone who, seeing all these works of God, does not praise Him, he is dumb; if there is anyone who, from so many signs, cannot perceive God, that man is foolish." — St. Bonaventure

Mountains and all hills,
fruit trees and all cedars!

Beasts and all cattle,
creeping things and flying birds!

"Thanks be to God for his inexpressible gift!"

— 2 Corinthians 9:15

Kings of the earth and all peoples,
princes and all rulers of the earth!

Young men and maidens together,
old men and children!

"A Christian should be an alleluia from head to foot."

— St. Augustine

Let them praise the name of the Lord,
for his name alone is exalted;
his glory is above earth and heaven.

"Whoever has God lacks nothing; God alone suffices."

— St. Teresa of Ávila

He has raised up a horn for his people,
praise for all his saints,
for the people of Israel who are near
to him.

Praise the LORD!

"Every morning prepare your soul for a tranquil day."

— St. Francis de Sales

Morning Offering

by Fr. Francois-Xavier Gautrelet

O Jesus, through the Immaculate Heart of Mary, I offer you all my prayers, works, joys, and sufferings of this day, for all the intentions of your Sacred Heart, in union with the Holy Sacrifice of the Mass throughout the world, in reparation for my sins, for the intentions of all my relatives and friends, and in particular for the intentions of the Holy Father.

"Faith is the door to the full inner life of the Church, a life which includes not only access to an authoritative teaching but above all to a deep personal experience which is at once unique and yet shared by the whole Body of Christ, in the Spirit of Christ."

— Thomas Merton

Act of Faith

O my God, I firmly believe that you are one God in three divine Persons, Father, Son, and Holy Spirit. I believe that your divine Son became man and died for our sins and that he will come to judge the living and the dead. I believe these and all the truths which the Holy Catholic Church teaches, because you have revealed them, who can neither deceive nor be deceived. In this faith I intend to live and die. Amen.

"Mercy is a gift of God the Father who is revealed in the Son. God's mercy gives rise to joyful gratitude for the hope which opens up before us in the mystery of our redemption by Christ's blood." — Pope Francis

Act of Hope

O my God, relying on your almighty power and infinite mercy and promises, I hope to obtain pardon for my sins, the help of your grace, and life everlasting, through the merits of Jesus Christ, my Lord and Redeemer.

"Everything comes from love, all is ordained for the salvation of man, God does nothing without this goal in mind." — St. Catherine of Siena

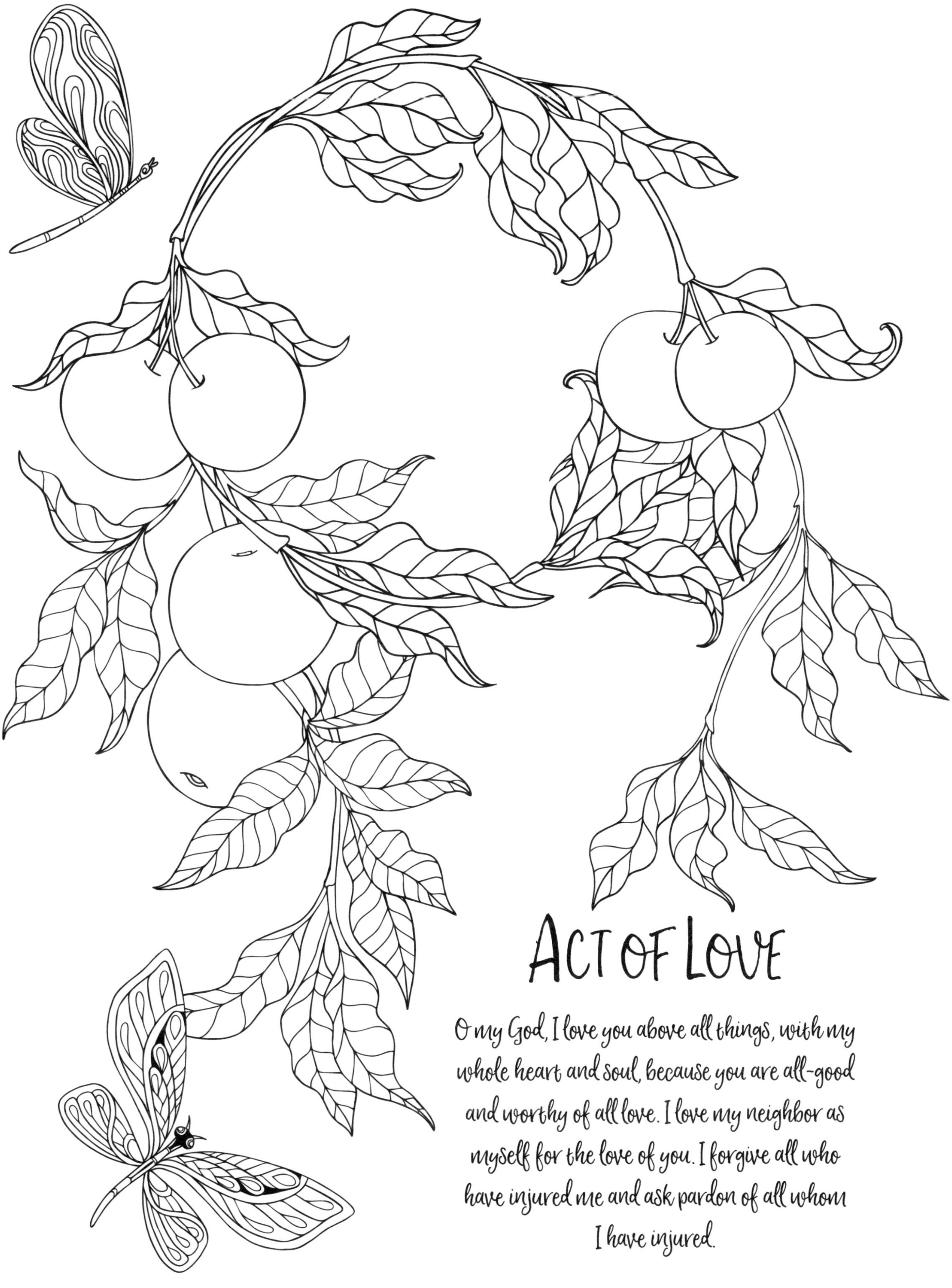

Act of Love

O my God, I love you above all things, with my whole heart and soul, because you are all-good and worthy of all love. I love my neighbor as myself for the love of you. I forgive all who have injured me and ask pardon of all whom I have injured.

"The soul should not dwell on the gifts, but on the Giver."

— St. Paul of the Cross

Holy, Holy, Holy Lord

Holy, Holy, Holy Lord God of hosts.
Heaven and earth are full of your glory.
Hosanna in the highest.
Blessed is he who comes in the name of the Lord.
Hosanna in the highest.

"O sinner, be not discouraged, but have recourse to Mary in all your necessities. Call her to your assistance, for such is the divine will that she should help in every kind of necessity." — St. Basil the Great

The Magnificat

(Luke 1:46-55)

"All the sins of your life seem to be rising up against you. Don't give up hope! On the contrary, call your holy mother Mary, with the faith and abandonment of a child. She will bring peace to your soul." — St. Josemaría Escrivá

My soul magnifies the Lord,
and my spirit rejoices in God my Savior,
for he has regarded the low estate of his handmaiden.

"He who knows how to forgive prepares for himself many graces from God. As often as I look upon the cross, so often will I forgive with all my heart."

— St. Faustina

For behold, henceforth all generations will call me blessed;
for he who is mighty has done great things for me,
and holy is his name.

"Prayer is not asking. Prayer is putting oneself in the hands of God, at his disposition, and listening to his voice in the depth of our hearts." — St. Teresa of Calcutta

And his mercy is on those who fear him
from generation to generation.

"Do not give your heart to that which does not satisfy your heart."

— St. Poemen

He has shown strength with his arm,
he has scattered the proud in the imagination
of their hearts,

"Joy is based on the spiritual knowledge that, while the world in which we live is shrouded in darkness, God has overcome the world."

— Henri J. M. Nouwen

he has put down the mighty from their thrones,
and exalted those of low degree;
he has filled the hungry with good things,
and the rich he has sent empty away.

"Let us never tire of prayer."

— St. Gaspar del Bufalo

He has helped his servant Israel,
in remembrance of his mercy,
as he spoke to our fathers,
to Abraham and to his posterity for ever.

"To cling always to God and to the things of God — this must be our major effort, this must be the road that the heart follows unswervingly."

— St. John Cassian

The Little Litany

Heart of my Creator, perfect me.
Heart of my Redeemer, answer for me.

"It is better to pray devoutly for your neighbor than to rebuke him every time he sins." — St. Mark the Ascetic

Heart of my Father, govern me.
Heart of my Judge, pardon me.
Heart of my Advocate, plead for me.

"The same everlasting Father who cares for you today will take care of you tomorrow and every day. He will either shield you from suffering or give you unfailing strength to bear it." — St. Francis de Sales

Heart of my Master, teach me.
Heart of my Pastor, guard me.
Heart of my faith Friend, rest in me.

"O Sacred Heart of Jesus, fountain of eternal life, Your Heart is a glowing furnace of Love. You are my refuge and my sanctuary."

— St. Gertrude the Great

Heart wounded for my love, receive me.
Sacred Heart of Jesus dying
on the Cross, save me.

"And I knew that the Spirit that had gone forth to shape the world and make it live was still alive in it." — Wendell Berry